This Book Belongs To

_____

SHELL YEAR
TREASUREBOOK

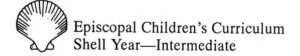

Episcopal Children's Curriculum
Shell Year—Intermediate

Developed by
Virginia Theological Seminary
Center for the Ministry of Teaching
3737 Seminary Road
Alexandria, VA 22304

Published by
Morehouse Publishing
P.O. Box 1321
Harrisburg, PA 17105

To Order Additional Copies
Call or Write:

MOREHOUSE PUBLISHING
Harrisburg, PA
Toll Free: 1-800-877-0012

ISBN: 0-8192-6016-9

Printed in the United States of America

Fourth Printing, 2002

Table of Contents

PART I
The Old Testament Story

1. Our God Speaks

Most of us know the names of people in the Bible, and we remember stories about them. But sometimes the Scriptures seem to be more of a riddle than a clear message. How would you explain what the Bible is? What makes it different from other books?

The heart of the Bible can be summed up in two words:

God speaks.

In this book we have a record of how God is made known to us. In the Bible we learn that God speaks and works through great deeds of people, and through the words of persons who explain and interpret. The very heart and mind of God are found in the words spoken to a chosen people.

God still speaks through the Scriptures to show us what life is all about. God speaks an answer to the problem of our sin. God gives us the good news that "true light" has come into our lives. That is why we call the Bible the Word of God.

One God, One People

From the Bible we learn that there is only one true God, not many gods. We read about individuals to whom God spoke—persons like Abraham, Isaac, Jacob (Israel), Moses, Miriam, and Deborah. They did what God asked them to do, and from them came a people known as the Twelve Tribes of Israel.

The Bible's story of the chosen people is filled with ups and downs. They had great gifts for doing good. But they also disobeyed God and failed to carry out their mission. The Bible is a record of their successes and failures, and their victories and defeats. God did not choose them to be pampered favorites. Israel was to be God's suffering servant to bless the world.

Special Voices

We would never be able to understand the Bible without the voices of leaders called *prophets, priests,* and *kings,* who speak through its pages. These persons, beginning with Moses and continuing to the time of John the Baptist, heard words from God. By the Holy Spirit they were inspired. They knew what God wanted in the world, and how God's people were meant to live.

These chosen leaders and speakers helped the people of God to establish times of prayer and worship in the Tabernacle and the Temple. They helped to give people patterns for living together—and with neighboring nations.

When the people disobeyed and went astray, as they so often did, it was the prophets who called them back to God.

God Speaks in Jesus Christ

For Christian readers of the Bible, everything in the Hebrew Scriptures (Old Testament) points toward the coming of Jesus Christ. In him, God speaks the final word which is loving good news for all humanity. From the New Testament we learn:

God *sent* Jesus Christ.

God is *like* Jesus Christ.

God is *in* Jesus Christ.

The resurrection of Jesus from the death he suffered on the cross was the proof that he was truly the Word "made flesh." The risen Christ becomes Lord in a new community in the world, the Church. He is Prophet, Priest, and King—all in one.

3

From the Gospels and Epistles, we learn how the same Holy Spirit who was there at the Creation, and in the life of Israel and its prophets, is now at work in the lives of Christian believers like ourselves.

The Holy Scriptures, then, are the very voice of God in every time and place, reminding us that we are forgiven for our sins and have hope of life everlasting.

It is also important to say what the Bible is *not*. It is not like a reference book we study only to get information. It is not a science book to explain our world. It is not even a history book, although it contains a lot of history. Not everything in the Bible is of equal importance, for it contains many different kinds of writing.

Some of the Bible is storytelling. Some is poetry and song. The Bible shares many detailed and ancient laws. And the Scriptures include records of bad deeds and violence that we might wish were not there.

But when we read and listen to the Bible as *a living book in which God speaks,* we can say that it is like a personal *letter* addressed to each of us. The Bible carries the name and address of every group and each person in the nations of the world.

Through the Bible, in every time and place, the living God has something to say to you and me. What God says makes all the difference in our lives!

2. One Bible in Many Languages

How many Bibles have you seen?

Bibles are everywhere—in our homes, in our churches and schools, in all kinds of libraries, even in hotel rooms. They are all sizes and shapes, printed in many ways. The Bible is available in more languages than any other book.

During the first centuries of American history, everyone who spoke and read English would expect the Bible to be the King James Version, first published in 1611. The language was the best of its day. To modern readers it sounds quite different from our ways of speaking. Pronouns like "thee" and "thou" were on every page. You could expect words like "shalt" for "shall," "holpen" for "helped," and "charity" for "love."

New Translations Help

In the twentieth century, many new versions and translations of the Bible have appeared—such as the Revised Standard Version, the New English Bible, the Good News Bible, the Jerusalem Bible, the New American Bible—and recently, the New Revised Standard Version. All of these help modern readers to understand more easily, since the language is more like our own.

Translators of the Bible must be good scholars of *Hebrew* in order to put the Old Testament (or Hebrew Scriptures) into other languages. They must be good scholars of *Greek* to do the same with the New Testament.

More than that, translators of the Bible have to think about how people interpret words in each day and time.

For example, consider the words of Jesus found in *Matthew 5:15*:

The **King James Bible** reads, "Neither do men light a candle, and put it under a bushel, but on a candlestick; and it giveth light unto all that are in the house."

The **New English Bible**, published in England in 1961, translates that verse, "When a lamp is lit, it is not put under the meal-tub, but on the lamp-stand, where it gives light to everyone in the house."

Americans did not find "meal-tub" better than "bushel." Here is how the verse reads in the **New Revised Standard Version**, published in the United States in 1989: "No one after lighting a lamp puts it under the bushel basket, but on the lampstand, and it gives light to all in the house."

So it goes. Different translators have struggled to help us hear, in our own tongue, the words first put down in Hebrew and Greek.

Sometime you might want to invite friends to share several translations of the Scriptures. Ask each person to read aloud a familiar chapter while the others follow in their own Bibles. Keep track of all the differences. Does it help us to understand when we compare in this way?

Many Centuries of Work

The story of how we got our Bible covers many hundreds of years. Have you wondered when it all began?

Since about 250 BCE (Before the Common Era), scholars have worked to make the Bible available to people in their own languages all over the world.

1. The Hebrew Old Testament
We cannot discover exact dates for the first written words of the Hebrew Old Testament. They were put

6

down on pieces of skin carefully prepared and sewn together, then rolled into scrolls. Many writers and editors worked with the text through the years, and copies were made by persons called scribes. For centuries, the scribes took great care not to make mistakes.

The first Hebrew Scriptures were written only with consonants. Jewish readers knew how to supply the vowels as they read. Later, Jewish scholars called Masoretes recognized that there would be errors in interpreting unless the vowels were added to the text. So they set about doing this. They relied on scholars in both Babylonia and Palestine, and their work was finished about 700 CE. This was the end of perhaps 500 years of labor to establish an authorized Hebrew Bible.

None of the original manuscripts still exists. The earliest copies of the complete Old Testament are preserved in the Middle East and in Russia. They are at least 1,000 years old.

2. The Greek New Testament

Original manuscripts of the New Testament, in Greek, are also lost. Scholars have compared copies that survive from the early centuries of the Church's history, and they have been able to establish an accepted text.

Some of the preserved fragments of the New Testament were written on papyrus (made from pressed fiber of reeds), and they are as old as the second and third centuries. These are now in libraries in England and America. The finest of the old manuscripts that were written on parchment or vellum, are in the Vatican in Rome and in the British Museum in London.

3. The Septuagint and the Vulgate

The Hebrew Scriptures were translated into Greek

over a period of three centuries just before Jesus was born. We call this translation the Septuagint. This Greek and Latin word meant "the Seventy." According to tradition, the Septuagint was produced by 70 (or 72) Jewish scholars—six from each of the twelve tribes of Israel.

Christians of the Roman Empire translated the Bible into Syriac, Armenian, Georgian, Coptic, Ethiopic, Gothic, Slavonic, and Arabic. But later, the Roman Catholic Church chose to oppose translation of the Scriptures in any language except *Latin*.

The Septuagint was translated into Latin, in several different versions. Pope Damascus of Rome was concerned because so many varying texts of the Bible were appearing. He appointed a scholar named Jerome to prepare a new Bible in Latin.

Jerome finished the New Testament over a ten-year period ending in 391 CE. Then, in order to translate the Old Testament, he moved to Bethlehem and studied Hebrew. He worked from 390 until 405, and at last the whole Bible was then in Latin. His beautiful translation is called the Vulgate.

For this great achievement, we honor St. Jerome each year on September 30, the date of his death in 420.

First English Bibles

A thousand years after Jerome's day, many English-speaking people wanted to be able to read the Bible in their own language.

Wycliffe Bible. The first complete English Bible was translated from the Latin Vulgate, by John Wycliffe about 1382-1383.

Tyndale Bible. In 1525, William Tyndale—working in Germany where he had gone to escape persecution—published a translation of the New Testament in English. Later, he translated the first five books of the Old Testament, and the book of Jonah. In 1536, he was burned at the stake as a heretic.

Coverdale Bible. There was no stopping the move to produce a complete English Bible. Miles Coverdale's version was finished in 1535. He used much of Tyndale's language, but the Psalms were his own work. We still use a version of Coverdale's Psalms in the Psalter of *The Book of Common Prayer*.

Matthew's Bible. In 1537, a new Bible appeared bearing the name of Thomas Matthew. It is believed that this was a pen name for John Rogers, who was an associate of William Tyndale.

Great Bible. Next came the Great Bible, also known as the Bible of Archbishop Thomas Cranmer because he wrote an introduction for it. It was a revision of Matthew's Bible, and it appeared in seven editions in the two years between 1539 and 1541.

Geneva Bible. Under Queen Mary (1553-1558), the English Bibles in the churches were gathered and burned. But a group of Puritan Christians had fled to Geneva, Switzerland, where they set about preparing another Bible. It is called the Geneva Bible and was finished in 1560.

The Geneva Bible included some of Tyndale's work, and some of the Great Bible. For the first time, the Bible was divided into *chapters* and *verses*.

King James Bible. Other English Bibles, both Protestant and Roman Catholic, were produced in the sixteenth and early seventeenth centuries. But the great Authorized Version was prepared in the time of King James I. He ordered that the Bible should be a good translation from the original languages of Hebrew and Greek. It was published in 1611, and was used for 250 years before British and American scholars began to produce the newer versions we now have.

It is hard to imagine a time when all readers could not have Bibles of their own. But for centuries, English Bibles were not published in large quantities so that individuals could own them. That would have been far too expensive for people to afford. Most of the Bibles were placed in churches, chained there permanently so that they would not be taken away.

We honor all the Christians who have given their lives so that we can have the Holy Bible. Truly the Scriptures are our most precious treasure, and we thank God for it.

3. The Books of the Old Testament

We call the Bible a book, and it looks like just one book with many pages. But the Bible is actually a series of books, some longer than others. It took hundreds of years for Jewish and Christian leaders to decide which books belong in the Bible, and in what order.

Thirty-nine books make up the Old Testament. We speak of them as the Hebrew "canon." (Canon means "rule" or "standard.") These Scriptures are arranged differently in Jewish and Christian Bibles.

The Jewish Bible

In Jewish Bibles, the thirty-nine books form three groups:

1. *The Torah* is the first five books—Genesis, Exodus, Leviticus, Numbers, and Deuteronomy. The Greek name for them is the Pentateuch. (The "penta" is from the word for five.)

Torah comes from a Hebrew word that means "to teach." We can say that the holy books of the Torah are teachings from God. Sometimes they are called the books of the Law because they contain the Ten Commandments and all the rules for the Hebrew people.

The Torah took its present form around 400 BCE.

2. *The Prophets* were divided into groups called Early and Later. The Early Prophets were Joshua, Judges, I and II Samuel, and I and II Kings. The Later ones were the books of Isaiah, Jeremiah, Ezekiel, Hosea, Joel, Amos, Obadiah, Jonah, Micah, Nahum, Habakkuk, Zephaniah, Haggai, Zechariah, and Malachi.

All these books found their way into the Scriptures through several centuries until around 200 BCE.

3. *The Writings* are a group of sacred books, most of which were already in existence before the canon of the prophets was established. These, in the order of their appearance, are: Psalms, Proverbs, Job, Song of Songs, Ruth, Lamentations, Ecclesiastes, Esther, Daniel, Ezra, Nehemiah, and I and II Chronicles.

This collection was brought together by 132 BCE.

It was about 90 CE, at the Rabbinical Council of Jamnia, when the final Old Testament canon was fixed as it now stands in Jewish Bibles.

11

The Christian Old Testament

In the Christian Bible, the Old Testament books are somewhat rearranged. The Pentateuch (Torah) remains the same. The prophets are placed last.

The other writings have been divided and shifted to new positions:

• The Book of Ruth was placed between Judges and I Samuel.

• I and II Chronicles, Ezra, Nehemiah, and Esther were moved up to follow II Kings.

• Lamentations was inserted just after Jeremiah.

• Daniel was included with the prophets, just after Ezekiel.

• The books of poetry (Job, Psalms, Proverbs, Ecclesiastes, and The Song of Solomon) were inserted just before the prophets.

In some modern Bibles, the Table of Contents for the Old Testament shows how the Christian canon has been organized. Here are the headings:

Pentateuch (Genesis through Deuteronomy; five books).

The Historical Books (Joshua through Esther; eleven books).

The Poetical Books (Job through The Song of Solomon; five books).

The Major Prophets (Isaiah, Jeremiah, Lamentations, Ezekiel, and Daniel; five books).

The Minor Prophets (Hosea through Malachi; thirteen books).

The Great Ideas

The Old Testament has a rich variety of writings. But running all through the books are some large ideas that hold it all together. These are:

The love of God. God made everything in the world and loved all creatures.

The justice of God. God cared about how people live and treat one another, desiring that people act justly and with mercy.

The teachings of God in the Torah. Here we read of the covenants God made with Noah, with Abraham and his family, and with Moses. The Ten Commandments were God's special gift to the chosen people. Their whole life was to be governed by them.

The promised land. God had led the people out of slavery in Egypt to a new home in Canaan. This was to be their land forever.

It was these four large ideas that led to the writing of the Hebrew Scriptures. The books centered around the *story* of the chosen people, Israel. Surrounding the story were rules of life, instructions for prayer and worship, important sayings, and other writings to inspire God's people. The Psalms were their prayer book and hymnal.

No matter how many times we read and study the Old Testament, we can always find something new to think about. And it is exciting to remember that Jesus also knew these same Scriptures and loved them.

4. The Pentateuch

The Hebrew people have always been storytellers. For a long time before they began to write things down, they handed down their great tales through many generations.

No doubt the stories were much longer, with many details, when they were shared aloud. The Biblical writers wanted to be sure the important points were saved; their accounts are like broad outlines to serve as the basis for family storytelling.

For example, in telling the story of Abraham and Sarah when they learned that they would have a son in their old age, it would be quite all right to add descriptions of Sarah—how she looked, how she sounded when she laughed, and what she said to her servants about the news. Such details would make the story more lively. The central theme would be clear: God surprised the couple by giving them the child, Isaac.

The first five books of the Bible, which we call the Torah or Pentateuch, include stories that taught the great truths every Hebrew child needed to know:

Genesis. The word "genesis" means "beginning." From this book we learn that the one true God made everything and called it "good." One story of Creation is told in *ch. 1.* It tells, in order, how God made the world and all creatures in six days. The seventh day was a Sabbath, a day of rest for God. (That is why God's people still observe sabbaths, times of refreshing and renewal.)

In a second Creation story, *chs. 2-3,* we learn that people spoiled the good creation by disobeying God. They sinned, and their sin made life corrupt.

Through a covenant with Noah, God made a new beginning after the Great Flood, *chs. 6-9.* The world was washed clean, and people had a fresh opportunity to obey God. But the problem of sin did not go away, as we can see through all the rest of the Bible.

God has never stopped loving his people. He called out Abraham to be parent to a new family of faith upon the earth. We can trace the long story of the descendants of Abraham and Sarah—Isaac, Jacob and Esau, and the children of Jacob (whose name had been changed to Israel). See *chs. 12-37.*

In a way, the most exciting stories are about Joseph, son of Jacob, who rose to be a great leader in Egypt and saved his people from famine and disaster, *chs. 37-50.*

From the Genesis stories we get a picture of the idea of "covenant" as a solemn agreement between God and the chosen people. God promises to be with them, and they promise to be faithful. God never breaks the covenant even when the people fall short and rebel.

Exodus. At the beginning of this book, the Hebrew people are still in Egypt. But a long time has passed since the end of the Genesis stories. The situation has changed drastically. The Egyptians do not remember Joseph. The descendants of Jacob have grown in numbers, and they are now considered a problem.

Here begins the long story of Moses, a Hebrew child who is saved from death through the cleverness of his mother and sister.

Moses grew up in the household of Pharaoh, but he did not forget that he was a Hebrew. When he saw one of his people being mistreated, he committed a murder and had to flee to the land of Midian in the Arabian peninsula. There he married Zipporah and tended flocks for his father-in-law, Jethro.

In time, Moses had a vision of a burning bush that was not consumed. From the bush God called to him, and Moses knew that he must be the one to lead the children of Israel to a Promised Land. See *ch. 3.*

It was difficult for the people of God to escape their sufferings in Egypt. Pharaoh was stubborn about allowing them to leave. Even after a series of terrible plagues, he refused. It was only following the great Passover that the people were permitted to leave. Pharaoh changed his mind and sent chariots of men to bring them back, but miraculously the Hebrews passed through the parted waters of the Red Sea. Their pursuers were destroyed, and the people were free at last. See *chs. 5-15.*

For forty years, Moses led the people in the wilderness. God provided manna for food and water from a rock. God was with the people the whole time even though they complained.

It was not easy for Moses to maintain order and justice among the people, even with the help of his brother, Aaron, and his sister, Miriam. God called Moses to Mt. Sinai, where he was given Ten Commandments. See *ch. 20.*

Imagine Moses' consternation when he returned and found that the people had fashioned a golden calf and were worshiping this idol in place of God! He was so angry that he broke the tablets on which the Commandments were written. He had to make another trip up the mountain to get the Commandments once again. See *chs. 32-34.*

The remainder of Exodus includes many additional laws. Directions are given for creating an ornamental box called an Ark of the Covenant, to contain the precious Commandments and to remind the people of the presence of God.

In *chs. 35-40* we can read about the building of the Tabernacle, a tent for the people's worship during their days in the desert.

Leviticus. This third book of the Pentateuch is almost entirely laws. God spoke to the people, saying, "You shall be holy; for I the Lord your God am holy" *(ch. 19:2)*. Almost all of the laws and regulations in Leviticus have to do with the people's worship.

For modern readers, the instructions for sacrificing animals seem quite strange. But many of the passages in this book are still useful for moral guidance, and for reminding us of the importance of prayer and worship.

In Philadelphia, at the shrine we call Independence Hall, the Liberty Bell has words from Leviticus around its surface: "Proclaim liberty throughout all the land unto all the inhabitants thereof." That is *Leviticus 25:10,* King James Version.

Numbers. The Hebrew name for this book is "In the Wilderness," a title that seems quite appropriate. The name, "Numbers," in the Christian Bible, comes from *chs. 1-4* and *ch. 26,* which tell of two numberings (census-takings) of the Hebrew people.

The other thirty-one chapters of the book are a history of Moses and the people of Israel as they lived in the wilderness. In *chs. 10-20,* we can read the story of a long journey from Sinai to Kadesh-barnea, on the way to Canaan.

Twelve spies were sent ahead to find out about conditions in Canaan. When they got back, Caleb and Joshua wanted the Hebrews to enter and conquer Canaan right away. But the people, like the ten other spies, were afraid. The result was a lengthened stay in the wilderness—forty years altogether.

In a final section of the book, *chs. 20-36,* a new generation of Israelites began an advance into Canaan. The tribes of Reuben, Gad, and half of Manasseh settled east of the Jordan River in Gilead. The other nine and a half tribes camped across the river from Jericho.

The book of Numbers ends with the story of Moses' death. He had not been allowed to enter the promised land.

Deuteronomy. The name of this book comes from Greek, and it means "second law." Deuteronomy retells the giving of the law and provides the Code that was intended to make Israel a nation of "one God, one altar, one people."

When Jesus was asked to name the greatest of all commandments *(Matthew 22:36-37),* he quoted from *Deuteronomy 6:5:* "You shall love the Lord your God with all your heart, and with all your soul, and with all your might." This has been called the best-loved verse in the Old Testament. All of *ch. 6:4-9* is known as the Shema (from the first word of the passage in Hebrew, meaning "hear").

Most of the book is arranged in the form of three long addresses by Moses, in Moab just before crossing the Jordan River. Along with all the rules and regulations, stories from the history of God's people are included.

In *ch. 34,* we learn again about Moses' death. Joshua was to be the new leader of Israel.

5. Outlines of Hebrew History

Following the death of Moses, the history of the Hebrews over the next eight hundred years falls into a series of stages:

• The people, under Joshua and the long line of judges that followed him, were a "theocracy" (ruled by God), and this marked them out as quite different from their neighboring tribes and nations.

• Following the period of judges, the people desired and were granted their first king, whose name was Saul. He was succeeded by the great King David. The next king was David's son, Solomon, who built the first Temple in Jerusalem. Under these three kings, Israel was one nation.

• What followed was a time of division, with Israel in the north, and Judah in the south. Lines of kings ruled over the divided peoples. Again and again their lives reflected both their faith in God and their tendency to rebel and go astray.

• Both Israel and Judah came upon hard times. The kingdom of Israel fell. The Babylonians captured the people of Judah and took them away from their land, destroying homes and laying waste the Temple.

• Under Cyrus, king of Persia, the people were allowed to begin their return from exile. They could look forward to renewing their worship and continuing their mission as the covenant people of God.

• The Temple was reconstructed, and the walls of Jerusalem were rebuilt.

This whole story unfolds in the Old Testament books of Joshua, Judges, I and II Samuel, I and II Kings, Ezra, and Nehemiah. Actually, the four books of Samuel-Kings are one long story covering about 500 years. Ezra and Nehemiah are probably one book that was later divided.

This section of the Bible would make a modern volume of more than 200 pages, but it is quite different from a history textbook. Every part of the story is intended to declare that God was working through leaders and events to work out a special purpose for the chosen people.

Book by book, here is what we can expect to find as we work our way through this history:

Joshua. Moses died around 1250 BCE, and it was up to his successor, Joshua, to lead in the further conquest of Canaan. At the beginning of his leadership, men, women, children, and their flocks of animals crossed the Jordan River and moved toward Jericho, twelve miles beyond. This city of six acres surrounded by walls, and occupied by about 1,500 people, was conquered.

Thus began a long, complicated, and very bloody period. By the time Joshua was buried in the ancient home of Abraham, he had won great victories and had kept the Hebrews together as God's own people.

Of special interest is *ch. 24,* where we can read Joshua's farewell address and also learn that God renewed the covenant with Israel.

Judges. The story of the conquest and settlement of Canaan continues in this book. The people were still living as tribes, without a strong central government. The "judges" who took over tribal leadership were not like our modern judges, although they did sometimes intervene to settle disagreements. They were tribal heroes who made war and who defended the Hebrews against the Canaanites and other invaders.

One of the fourteen judges described in the book was a woman. Deborah has been called a sort of Biblical Joan of Arc. Her song in the Book of Judges is considered one of the oldest pieces of writing in the Old Testament. She called for 40,000 volunteers to destroy the army of Canaan. Only 10,000 responded, but she directed Barak, a warrior, to attack. They were victorious, and Deborah sang her song in response.

All through the stories of the judges in Israel, we can see a familiar pattern. The people knew that they were to serve God, but they failed again and again. God had to try over and over to teach the people the lesson of obedience.

Also clear in Judges is the teaching that the victories of the Hebrews were not due to the power of any human leader. Only by the power of God were they able to prevail. The stories are not pleasant to read. Some of the judges were cruel and did wicked things. But the Bible shares the whole story of their faults as well as their achievements.

Here are the names of the fourteen judges: Othniel, Ehud, Shamgar, Deborah, Barak, Gideon, Abimelech, Tola, Jair, Jephthah, Ibzan, Elon, Abdon, and Samson. They ruled from about 1200 to 1020 BCE.

I and II Samuel. The first seven chapters of the book of I Samuel tell the story of Samuel, the last judge in Israel. He had succeeded the aging Eli, who had been a weak leader.

At his birth, Samuel had been dedicated by his parents, Elkanah and Hannah, to the service of God. When he was a young child, they took Samuel to live in Shiloh, a short distance north of Jerusalem. When he was twelve, he heard the call of God, and he committed himself to a faithful life as leader among his people. He lived to a ripe old age and was probably the greatest of Israel's judges.

It was Samuel who responded to the people's desire for a king who would bring stronger leadership to Israel. At God's direction, Samuel anointed Saul to be the first monarch. Samuel tried hard to help Saul be a good king.

When it was clear that Saul was not mentally stable and able to lead, Samuel anointed David—shepherd boy and son of Jesse—to be the next king. See *I Samuel 16:1-13.*

David was designated to follow Saul, but Saul was still the king. David and Saul's son, Jonathan, became very close friends. Saul tried to have David killed, but Jonathan pleaded for David's life. Then David and Jonathan made a covenant with each other and went their separate ways. (See *chs. 18-20.*)

For a time, David was a fugitive living in the countryside in order to escape Saul. At one point, David had a chance to kill Saul, but he spared his life. (See *ch. 26.*)

At the end of I Samuel, Saul was defeated by the Philistines. He and his sons died in battle, *ch. 31.*

II Samuel begins with a song in which David, the musician and poet, laments the death of Saul and Jonathan. It is called The Song of the Bow.

The main events that follow have to do with David's life as king over all Israel. His reign was a time of strength and pride for the people. He brought the Ark of the Covenant to Jerusalem and made that city the center of worship for the Hebrews.

David fell in love with a woman named Bathsheba, the wife of Uriah. Arranging to have Uriah killed in battle, David took Bathsheba as his own wife. A prophet named Nathan rebuked David strongly for what he did, and David knew that he had sinned greatly. He and Bathsheba had a son named Solomon. (See *chs. 11-12.*)

Absalom, a son of David, rebelled. He won the people away from David and even drove David out of Jerusalem. But when Absalom was killed in battle, David was overcome by grief, *ch. 18:9-33.*

In *ch. 22,* David sang a psalm of praise for victory. At last the Philistines were no longer a threat.

The two books of Samuel cover the period from about 1025 to 925 BCE.

I and II Kings. The first of these books begins with the death of David and the start of Solomon's kingship. By *ch. 11* the kingdom has reached its zenith. At the end of II Kings, it has nearly died. The tragedy of Israel's decline had to do with the character of Solomon.

When challenged by opponents, Solomon would simply have them banished or killed. He developed industry and trade so that he could acquire many stables, mines, and ships. But the people gained no share in this great wealth for which they toiled. They had to pay heavy taxes and to do forced labor.

Solomon built a Temple, and he is honored for that. He spoke eloquently at the dedication, *ch. 8.*

But the Temple was just one of many buildings Solomon erected; some were lavish palaces for himself, his many queens, and the court. The great building program took twenty years, and Solomon had to borrow very heavily. In the end he had to sacrifice twenty cities of Galilee to cover his debts.

Solomon's son, Rehoboam, was even less responsible. When he succeeded his father as king, he would not reduce the people's burdens. The result was a split of the kingdom in 922. A former labor leader, Jeroboam, became monarch over the northern kingdom known as Israel. Rehoboam was left with only the two tribes of Judah, in the southern kingdom.

The northern kingdom ended in 721. Judah lasted until 586, when many were carried into exile in Babylon. Of these deported people, a psalmist wrote, "By the waters of Babylon, there we sat down and wept, when we remembered Zion" *(Psalm 137:1)*.

Between 922 and 587, nineteen kings and one queen (Athaliah) ruled in Judah. Nineteen kings led Israel between 922 and 721.

In the books of the Kings we have the stories of two prophets, Elijah and Elisha, who wrote nothing but who had great faith. Elijah is noted for his challenge to the prophets of Baal and for his courage when threatened by Queen Jezebel. (See *I Kings, chs. 17-21* and *II Kings 2-5*.)

In II Kings, we can read about one good reform under King Josiah. When the temple was being repaired, Josiah's secretary, Shaphan, went to confer with Hilkiah, the priest, about the payroll for the workmen. Hilkiah showed Shaphan a scroll that had turned up in the temple. It was probably the Book of Deuteronomy—placed there earlier in the hope that it would be found.

Shaphan took the scroll to Josiah, and he was alarmed. Idol worship had been thriving in Judah, and the scroll pronounced God's judgment on such behavior. Josiah brought the people together and read the scroll aloud. He called on everyone solemnly to obey the Code they had just heard. (See *II Kings, chs. 22-23*.)

But Josiah did not live long enough to accomplish his reform. He was killed in battle in 609.

II Kings ends as Nebuchadnezzar of Babylonia takes Jerusalem, and Judah is led into exile.

Ezra and Nehemiah. In 597 and 587 BCE, some of the people of Judah were driven across the desert into their time of exile in Babylon. They managed to live with their captors and retain their identity. Then, in 538, Cyrus of Persia defeated Babylonia. Wherever Cyrus found deported persons, he gave them permission to return home. This happened as well for the Jews; they were allowed to return to Palestine and rebuild Jerusalem.

It was an 800-mile journey back to their own land. Only some of the exiles from Judah were willing to undertake the heavy work of travel and rebuilding. Some stayed behind in Babylon, and others returned to Palestine later.

The first group arrived in 536, with families, helpers, and equipment. They faced a daunting task. So much had been destroyed or left in ruins. Homes had to be built. But the people longed to have their Temple as well. They started work on it at once, and it took twenty years for them to finish.

In these two books of Ezra and Nehemiah, we can read about the following:

• The first return of the exiles.

• The completion of the temple, under a governor named Zerubbabel.

• The work of Nehemiah in rebuilding the walls of Jerusalem. He had been a cupbearer to the king of Persia, Artaxerxes. When the king discovered

Nehemiah's deep concern about the city of Jerusalem, he sent him there as governor with instructions to undertake the restoration of the walls. The task was accomplished in just fifty-two days. See especially *Nehemiah 8:1-12,* as the people heard the law. Nehemiah taught the people to observe their sabbath, *ch. 13:15-22.*

• The appearance of Ezra, a teacher and writer who helped the people to restore an orderly life of godly obedience. See especially *Ezra 7:1-10.* He was harsh, particularly when he moved to end mixed marriages between Jews and people of the land. But Ezra made a great contribution. He brought back a Torah scroll (books of the law of Moses) from Mesopotamia, and he made it the guiding book in the people's lives.

The period of Nehemiah and Ezra covers the time from 536 to about 425 BCE.

6. Four Books Tucked In, and More to Come

We have surveyed the long journey of Abraham's many descendants, and read of the mighty acts of God in the life of Israel. There is no more of this history in the Bible.

But the group of Historical Books in our Christian canon of Hebrew Scriptures includes the following four books:

I and II Chronicles
Ruth
Esther
Where do they fit in?

I and II Chronicles tell the same story that we find in the books of Samuel and Kings. They include long passages lifted from these earlier accounts. One difference is that the writer of Chronicles begins with Adam and concludes by dipping into the Persian period of history, which came after the Hebrews' return from the exile. Scholars believe the composer of Chronicles was the same person who wrote Ezra and Nehemiah.

These books do not add to our knowledge of the history of Israel. The writer has an intense desire to paint a good picture of the life of the Jewish people.

Ruth is a touching story set in the period of the judges. Ruth herself was a Moabite woman, whose husband was Mahlon, son of a Jewish couple—Elimelech and Naomi, who had gone to Moab to escape a famine in their native Judah. They were from Bethlehem. The husbands of both Naomi and Ruth died. Naomi decided to return to her own land, and Ruth insisted on going with her. We remember Ruth's tenderness and great loyalty.

In Bethlehem, the women were welcomed back graciously. Ruth gained favor with Boaz, who allowed her to pick grain in his fields. She and Boaz were married, and their son was Obed (a grandfather of King David). Ruth was an ancestor of Jesus.

This book was written around 500 BCE. It is a Hebrew "writing," a short story with a historical background.

Esther is another historical short story. It tells about a brave young woman who saved the Jewish people at a time when they were threatened in Persia. The Jewish

Feast of Purim celebrates the story. At this Feast, Esther's story is read aloud.

Probably written between 350 and 250 BCE, this book is treasured by the Jewish people because it speaks of their survival in times of persecution. Oddly, the name of God does not appear in the entire story.

Of Prophets and Poets

The remainder of the Old Testament is composed of writings from the prophets, and a collection of poetry, songs, and "wisdom literature."

The prophets' words must be studied against the backdrop of all the history we have surveyed in this Shell Year Treasurebook. Each prophet's message is related to the events described in the Pentateuch and the historical books that follow. We will explore all that they said and did, in other Treasurebooks.

PART II
The New Testament

1. The In-Between Times

When we turn, in our Bibles, from the Old Testament to the New Testament, we have just skipped over nearly five hundred years! What happened during all that time? Does it matter?

The Old Testament gives us a history of the Hebrews, God's chosen people. The story comes to an end around 432 BCE (Before the Common Era), when the great Persian Empire still controlled that part of the world.

The Persians had allowed the last of the Hebrews to return from exile. They rejoiced that they could once again live in Palestine with its beloved capital city of Jerusalem.

At the end of this Old Testament history, Ezra and Nehemiah rebuilt the walls of Jerusalem. These men also reorganized the life of the people around the Law of the Lord. Once again, the worship of God was at the center of everyday affairs.

Unfortunately, we do not know very much about the next two hundred years of Hebrew history.

In the outside world, great things were happening. Alexander the Great, of Macedonia, became master of the whole civilized world, and the Persian Empire crumbled. The Greek language and culture spread throughout Alexander's world.

After the sudden death of Alexander in 323 BCE, his empire was divided up by generals who struggled with one another. Finally, three kingdoms were established:

- Macedonia, located toward the west.
- Syria, reaching to the east.
- Egypt, the largest of the kingdoms, situated between the other two.

This three-way division lasted until late in the third century BCE. During this time, the Jewish territory of Palestine was part of the kingdom of Egypt. The Egyptian rulers were tolerant, and they seldom interfered with the lives of the Jewish people.

Struggle Against the Syrians

Then, just before 200 BCE, a new situation developed. The Egyptian kingdom began to grow weak. That led the kings of Syria to start gobbling up more territory for themselves. In the process, Syria grabbed Palestine away from Egypt.

At first, the Jews were delighted about the Syrians' victory. But soon they were disappointed. A Syrian leader named Antiochus, and his son, were unwilling to let the Jews live in peace. They wanted to impose the Greek language and Greek customs throughout their lands. The Jewish people resisted. They wanted to keep their own religion and way of life.

The Syrian leaders decided to force the Jews to obey them. In 168 BCE, Antiochus IV moved in and destroyed parts of their holy city, Jerusalem. He desecrated the temple. He tried to stamp out the Jewish religion completely.

The Jews, under the leadership of men called the Maccabees, began to fight back against the Syrians. Fierce battles continued for twenty years. (Sometimes the Maccabees also attacked other Jewish groups who wanted to cooperate with the Syrian enemy.)

Finally, in 142 BCE, the Jewish state at last was granted religious and political freedom. For almost a century the people enjoyed their independence.

Rome Rises to Power

But the world once again took a new turn. Rome became a strong power. The Syrians and the Egyptians had to worry about protecting themselves from the Romans, and they neglected the territory of Palestine.

Two rival leaders were struggling for rule over the Palestinian city of Jerusalem. In 63 BCE, they appealed to Rome for help. This turned out to be a foolish mistake. The Roman general, Pompey, seized the opportunity to march into Palestine and take over the whole area.

For more than a third of a century, the Jews were subject to a new set of petty rulers installed by the Romans. The most famous of these was Herod the Great.

For a while the Jewish patriots tried to resist, but it was no use. The Romans were too strong.

Life Under Rome

Jesus was born in Palestine during this time of Roman rule. Rome dominated a huge portion of the world, from North Africa and Spain to the Black Sea.

Anyone who wandered through Palestine in the days of Jesus might have imagined that this was part of Greece. The people spoke the Greek language, which had by now been imposed by the Romans. The cities were laid out like Greek cities. Each one had temples to the Greek gods, Zeus and Artemis. Cities also had theaters, forums with tall pillars, stadiums, gymnasiums, and public baths.

Only the many small towns and villages in the countryside of Galilee and Judah kept their Jewish style of building. It was in these real Jewish communities that Jesus lived and worked. He did not live in any of the truly Roman cities.

Still, the Jewish communities were affected by the Greek culture that Rome had promoted. Natives of

Galilee and Judah wore the same kinds of clothes that were worn in Alexandria, Rome, or Athens: a tunic and cloak, shoes or sandals, and a hat or cap.

Furniture in Jewish homes included a Greek-style bed, and the people adopted the Roman habit of eating while reclining.

One of the ways in which Rome kept control over its people was through the census. It served two purposes—to provide information for calling up men to serve in the military, and to help in collecting taxes from everyone.

For the Jewish people, the Roman taxes were a chief worry. The Romans collected the money in order to create beautiful buildings and keep up an extravagant life for leaders in the empire.

Roman emperors promised their people "bread and circuses." Egypt provided corn for the free bread. The great arenas for public games were built by slaves that were bought with tax money.

For a long time, the census was taken every five years. It was then abandoned for a long period. But the idea was revived by the emperor Caesar Augustus. It was under his rule that Quirinius, governor of Syria, carried out the census at the time of Jesus' birth *(Luke 2:1-2)*.

The Jewish Religion

During the many struggles of the Jewish people during the five hundred years between the Old Testament and the New Testament, four main developments seem to have occurred:

1. Ceremonies. Jewish life centered around the Temple and the priests. It was important to have daily sacrifices, with private offerings for special occasions and public sacrifices for the Day of Atonement and other great days. The rules and ceremonies for these times were very detailed and precise.

2. *The Law.* The Torah (Genesis, Exodus, Leviticus, Numbers, and Deuteronomy) became more and more important. Synagogues were growing in number because so many people were far from Jerusalem and could go to the Temple only on rare occasions. Members of the synagogues studied hard to memorize the Torah, explain it to one another, and hold it in high honor. It was absolutely essential to the unity of Jewish people.

3. *Wisdom.* Not only the Greeks and the Egyptians but also the Jews, came to treasure the wise sayings that had been preserved from leaders of the past. The Jewish leaders honored their own "wisdom" that had been collected and written down. One idea in the wisdom writings was very popular: that *evil* is always punished and *doing good* always brings reward.

4. *Expecting the "last days."* For centuries, the Jewish people had believed, especially in times of gloom, that God would take charge of world affairs. God would punish oppressors and support God's chosen people. This was the message of prophets who had announced that a Messiah would come. There would be a new Day of the Lord.

But in the Persian and Greek periods, new ideas began to creep into this pattern of Jewish thought. Using elaborate symbolic numbers and figures, some of the writers worked out a sensational way of looking at history. They said that God would act suddenly to restore the nation of Israel to a position of power.

What the people seemed to forget was that none of these four developments really matched what God wanted most. Again and again, through the Hebrew prophets of long ago, God had called on the people to reach out and share their faith with others. They were to be God's servants to the world.

Instead of heeding these calls, the people had focused too much on themselves, neglecting their larger mission.

2. A New Covenant

About the year 30 CE (Common Era), events in the city of Jerusalem changed the whole future of humankind.

The Jewish people were restless and discontented. They enjoyed a certain amount of independence under the Roman rulers. Still, they had a burning desire to be free from all foreign influence.

Priests and religious groups were very serious about worship in the Temple and keeping the Law (Torah). But many lacked a strong faith that God was really at work in the affairs of the world.

In the past, the people had been sure about the *covenant* God had made with Abraham. God had promised that Abraham's descendants would be as numerous as the stars. The Israelites were sure that Abraham and Sarah and their descendants had been chosen and led by none other than the very God of heaven and earth.

In the same way, the people had once been sure that God had made a great Covenant with Moses on Mt.

Sinai. The Commandments were a gift to the Hebrews and the whole world. The people had been saved, protected, and led by the direct action of God.

Now—after so many hundreds of years—the people were starved for news that God was still able to act powerfully in their midst. Some doubted that God would ever again be known in the same way as in times past.

Into this scene came a band of Jewish people who shouted good news: God had brought salvation at last! The living Spirit of God was in the very midst of them. A new age had come, and it was now time for people to turn to God and be saved.

This good news focused on Jesus of Nazareth.

In Jesus Christ, God had made a New Covenant. (New Covenant and New Testament have the same meaning.) It was an exciting story told first in Jerusalem, then in the rest of Palestine, and finally throughout the Roman empire. The story has been preserved for us in the New Testament of our Bibles.

3. The Written New Testament

Most of us go through a book by starting on the first page and following along to the end. That is certainly one way to read the New Testament. We can begin with the first verse of the Gospel of Matthew and read on to the last verse of Revelation.

But that may not be the best way to understand all these pages that have one big story to tell:

God came into the world and did something alto-gether new in a man named Jesus of Nazareth. This is great good news for us all.

Jesus was not just another great and wise person. He rose from the dead! He is still living as our Lord Jesus Christ. He is God in our midst.

Try opening the New Testament first to The Acts of the Apostles. It was written by Luke in order to trace the beginning of the Christian church.

In The Acts, we read first the story of Jesus' ascension into heaven after he promised his eleven apostles that they would receive the gift of the Holy Spirit. At once, the men chose Matthias to take the place of Judas who had betrayed Jesus. See *ch. 1*.

Then comes the dramatic story of Pentecost. Like flames of fire and with the rush of a mighty wind, the Holy Spirit descended upon the apostles, and they began to speak in a way that could be understood by people of many languages. See *ch. 2*.

Peter preached a sermon that helps us understand just how the early Church interpreted what Jesus Christ was all about. See *ch. 2:14-36*.

The Acts of the Apostles goes on to tell the story of all the things that happened to Peter, Paul, and the other apostles as the Church preached its message and attracted more and more people in the Roman empire.

Jesus Was Messiah

In The Acts of the Apostles, it is very clear that the first Christians knew Jesus was the promised *Messiah*.

"Messiah" means "anointed one." In ancient Hebrew

times, kings and priests were anointed with oil as they took up their work. The title of messiah was given to persons like Abraham and Isaac who were chosen to administer the rule of God among the people.

In time, David the king received a promise from God that his family would always rule over Israel. Later, prophets like Jeremiah, Micah, and Isaiah, spoke of a future day when a king in the royal line of David would come to be a great deliverer of the people. He would be the true Messiah of God—a person who had the power to save God's people and establish his rule forever.

The New Testament writers brought the good news that this expected Messiah had indeed come, and he was Jesus of Nazareth who died on a cross and was raised from the dead. He was not a king mighty in military conquest. He came instead as a lowly servant. Still, he was King of kings and Lord of lords:

• God who called Abraham was now present with God's people through the risen Lord Jesus.

• God who led the Hebrews out of slavery in Egypt, under the leadership of Moses, had now acted to save humankind from the power of sin and death.

• God who had spoken for so long through the prophets had now sent the promised One into the world.

• God in Christ had established a new age. He was seen to be Alpha and Omega, "the beginning and the end." (The first and last letters of the Greek alphabet are alpha and omega—and they have become a symbol for Jesus Christ as the ruler of all human history.)

When we finish reading Luke's account in The Acts, we are hungry to know more! We wonder when and how Jesus was born. We wonder what he said and did that caused Peter and the others to follow him. We wonder how he came to die. And most of all, we wonder how people knew that he was raised from the dead.

So our curiosity causes us to turn back to the four Gospels. There we can read four different writers' way of telling about Jesus the Messiah. The first three Gospels—Matthew, Mark, and Luke—are very much alike. John is different, as we shall see.

4. Mark, Matthew, and Luke

The first three Gospels report mostly the same words and acts of Jesus. Deeds of power, parables, conversations, and main events in his life are the same.

Because of the similarities in Mark, Matthew, and Luke, we call them "Synoptics." That is, they give a synopsis (summary) of the story of Jesus Christ. These Gospels were probably written between 65 and 90 CE, during the two generations after Jesus' resurrection.

People in the Church had passed along the stories of Jesus again and again without writing them down—just as families have always told about events without putting them on paper. Now, in the Gospels, writers were at last producing a record, in the Greek language, of what had previously been an "oral tradition."

In recent centuries, since the invention of printing, it has been possible to lay the Gospels alongside one another and draw parallels to show which lines are alike.

We can see that each of these Gospels includes some stories that do not appear in the other two. But almost all of Mark is also in Matthew or Luke, or both. This leads us to believe that Mark was written first, and the other two writers borrowed from his work.

Matthew and Mark agree on 170-180 verses. Luke and Mark share about 50 verses. All three Synoptics agree on about 350-370 verses!

But then we notice an interesting fact: Matthew and Luke agree on about 230 verses that are not found in Mark at all. Since they clearly did not borrow these from Mark, what happened?

Most Bible scholars believe Matthew and Luke also made use of a story of Jesus that has now disappeared. This mystery document is sometimes called "Q" (named for a German word, Quelle, that means "source").

General Outline

It is helpful to know that the Synoptics all include four general sections:

	Matthew	Mark	Luke
1. Events before Jesus' ministry begins	3:1-4:11	1:1-13	3:1-4:13
2. Jesus' ministry in Galilee	4:12-18:35	1:14-9:50	4:14-9:50
3. Jesus' journey to Jerusalem	19:1-20:34	10:1-52	9:51-18:43
4. Trial, death, and resurrection	chs. 21-28	chs. 11-16	chs. 19-24

The greater part of these Gospels, then, is devoted to the events of the two or three years of Jesus' ministry in Palestine. He traveled around in Galilee, Judea, Samaria, and Perea, doing the work God had sent him to do.

Parables and Miracles

Two things stand out: Jesus' teaching in *parables,* and his *healing miracles.*

• Again and again, Jesus' parables began, "The kingdom of God (heaven) is like . . . ." Then he would tell simple stories about a sower and seed, a woman searching her house for a coin, a shepherd with a flock, and a fisher with a great catch. Or he told stories about the arranging of a wedding, the building of a house, and the management of a household and its servants.

The parables seemed so simple. But they made a plain point about seeking the rule of God in every person's life and in the affairs of the world.

• The healing miracles of Jesus were deeds of great power. They were victories over forces of sin and death. They were never done just to be sensational, as the work of a magician would be. Instead, Jesus' miracles showed that God was present to heal people. They showed that God was loving and forgiving, and cared about the wounded and brokenhearted.

Jesus did not try to compel people to put their faith in him. He simply said, "Believe," or "Do not be afraid, only believe," or "Sin no more," or "Go home to your friends, and tell them what God has done for you."

As Luke put it, Jesus "went about doing good and healing all who were oppressed by the devil, for God was with him" *(Acts 10:38).*

Each Gospel Has a Purpose

Each of the Synoptics has a kind of special flavor. The writers had their own purposes in mind.

• **Mark** probably had no idea that he was beginning a form of writing that had never been done before, called a Gospel. He was simply trying to explain how the Church had come into being through the ministry, death, and resurrection of Jesus Christ. He wanted to explain why Christians are baptized, and why they gather for Eucharist. Above all, he wanted to preserve in writing what the Church was to proclaim to the world: A New Covenant had been established, and a new age had begun. The Holy Spirit of God was present in the Church.

• **Matthew** is an expanded edition of Mark's Gospel. The writer wanted to underscore the fact that Jesus was truly the expected Messiah for whom the Jewish people had waited. He provided a table of the ancestors of Jesus to show that he was a "son of David." Also, Matthew put Jesus' teachings into an order that people could recall, even memorize. See especially the Sermon on the Mount *(chs. 5-7)*, the great charge to declare God's rule to the world *(ch. 10)*, the parables of God's rule *(ch. 13)*, teaching on being humble and forgiving *(ch. 18)*, and Jesus' words about the end of the age *(chs. 24-25)*.

• **Luke** was a more polished writer than Mark and Matthew, but his Gospel follows Mark's outline. It is full of "good news of great joy." His story of the birth of Jesus begins with the happiness of Elizabeth and Zechariah when they had a son in their old age—John, who became the Baptist. Of course, his Gospel includes the sad and the ugly. But it ends with the great happiness of the disciples who gathered daily after the glad resurrection of Jesus, praising and blessing God.

Mark said nothing about Jesus' birth. To find the story

of Mary and Joseph and the stable in Bethlehem, we can turn only to Luke *(ch. 2)*. The story of the wise men and their visit to worship the Christ Child is found only in Matthew *(ch. 2)*. As we share the good news of Christmas each year, we piece these two stories together. We are grateful for the glimpse they provide into the beginning of our Lord's life.

5. The Fourth Gospel

The Gospel of John is quite different from the Synoptics. It was written later, probably around 90-100 CE, by an unidentified "beloved disciple."

If we did not have the Synoptics, we would not know for sure that John the Baptist baptized Jesus. The Gospel of John seems to assume that the story is well known; it speaks of John's work as baptizer and of the descending dove—but the actual baptism of Jesus in the Jordan is omitted.

And John also leaves out the words of Jesus at the Last Supper, "This is my body . . . ," and "This is my blood . . . ."

It may be that John had read the other Gospels, especially Mark, and assumed that readers of his own Gospel would not need to be told everything the others had already shared repeatedly.

Also, John shares no parables from Jesus. His Gospel includes teachings and long speeches but none of the short stories that began, "The kingdom of God is like . . . ."

The Gospel contains just seven miracles. Each was a "sign" of the new life that Jesus Christ was bringing into the world:

1. *Water changed to wine*. At a wedding feast in Cana, attended also by his mother, Jesus performed his first deed of power. The host was embarrassed by a lack of wine. Jesus produced many gallons of it by asking the servants to pour water into six large stone jars. See *ch. 2:1-11*.

2. *Healing an official's son*. A royal official from Capernaum begged Jesus to come to his home and heal his son who was near death. Jesus simply told him, "Go; your son will live." As the official started home, he was met by servants who gave him the good news that the son was recovering. See *ch. 4:46-54*.

3. *Healing a man on the sabbath*. In Jerusalem, a man who had been sick thirty-eight years was lying by the pool of Beth-zatha. The pool was supposed to have powers to cure. But the man had no one to help him get into the water at the proper time. When Jesus heard the man's story, he told him to pick up his mat and walk. To everyone's amazement, the man stood and began to walk. Religious leaders were displeased because Jesus performed this miracle on the sabbath day. See *ch. 5:1-18*.

4. *Feeding five thousand*. Great crowds were following Jesus by the Sea of Galilee. Evening came, and the disciples wondered how the people would be fed. With five loaves of bread and two fish, Jesus fed about five thousand people. Food was left over—enough to fill twelve baskets. See *ch. 6:1-15*.

5. *Walking on water*. After the feeding of the five thousand, the disciples got into a boat and headed across the sea to Capernaum. A strong wind came, and the men had to row hard for several miles. Then they saw Jesus walking toward them on the water. He said, "It is I; do not be afraid." The disciples wanted to take

Jesus into the boat, but just then they discovered they were on the shore! See *ch. 6:16-21.*

6. *Healing a blind man.* Jesus spat on the ground, made mud, and spread the mud on the eyes of a man born blind. He told the man to go and wash in the pool of Siloam. He did so, and immediately he was able to see. This miracle, too, was performed on the sabbath. Again, the religious authorities were very angry because Jesus disregarded the sabbath law. They drove Jesus away. See *ch. 9:1-34.*

7. *Raising of Lazarus.* Jesus learned that his dear friend, Lazarus, the brother of Martha and Mary, had died. Jesus wept. Then he performed his last and greatest sign. He stood before the tomb where the dead man had lain for several days and shouted, "Lazarus, come out!" To the great amazement of the mourners standing by, Lazarus appeared at the door of the tomb, wrapped in his burial clothes. He was alive again! See *ch. 11:1-44.*

All these signs together point to Jesus as the true Son of God, the Messiah. He had power over nature, power over the forces of sickness, evil, and darkness, and power over death itself.

Like an unfolding drama on a stage, the Gospel of John describes Jesus' ministry as a series of crises that will end with his being condemned to die on the cross. Cruel officials plot Jesus' death.

But through it all, we see in John's Gospel much that is tender and very touching—like the story of the woman named Mary who poured costly perfume on Jesus' feet and wiped them with her hair *(ch. 12:1-9).*

The story of the Last Supper, in John, is about Jesus' washing of the disciples' feet. He told them that he had come to be a servant, and that he wanted them to be servants as well. See *ch. 13*.

John's Gospel also shares a series of seven "I am . . . " statements that Jesus used to describe himself:

- "I am the bread of life" *(ch. 6:41-48)*.
- "I am the light of the world" *(chs. 8:12, 9:5)*.
- "I am the door (gate)" *(ch. 10:7-9)*.
- "I am the good shepherd" *(ch. 10:11-16)*.
- "I am the resurrection and the life" *(ch. 11:25)*.
- "I am the way, and the truth, and the life" *(ch. 14:6)*.
- "I am the vine" *(ch. 15:1-5)*.

Each of these statements opens up to us the greatness of our Lord Jesus Christ and all that he came to do for us.

Through this Gospel we hear the Holy Spirit declaring that Jesus was the Word of God that came among us as a living human being and brought us to newness of life through his death and resurrection. See *John 1:1-18*.

6. Scribes, Pharisees, and Sadducees

In the Gospels, the groups that were most critical of Jesus were the scribes, the Pharisees, and the Sadducees. And Jesus accused these men of a distorted kind of faith. Who were they? What were they like?

- The *scribes* were skilled at copying the Scriptures of the Jewish people. They set high standards for preserving these writings and for guarding against introducing false or foreign material.

Scribes in the Old Testament were like secretaries, keeping records on clay tablets.

But after the Jews returned from their exile in Babylon, scribes took on a new and more important role. People needed interpreters of the Torah, and the scribes became lay teachers who helped to do that. They were scholars, sages, and wise men.

Ezra, co-worker with Nehemiah in rebuilding the walls of Jerusalem, was said to be the first scribe to fill a religious role as well.

By the time of Jesus, scribes were numerous. They were religious lawyers, interpreting the Torah with precise arguments. They were opposed to Jesus because he questioned the great authority they assumed. See *Matthew 7:29*, for example. A few of them believed in Jesus, but many chose to stand against him.

• The *Pharisees* were a religious party whose name probably meant "separated." Thousands of them were living in the Jerusalem area in the time of Jesus.

They were students and teachers of the Law—both the Torah and the many oral codes by which the Jewish people lived. Although the New Testament speaks harshly of the Pharisees, we can be grateful to them for some of the things they accomplished. For example, they enlarged the Hebrew Scriptures to include the Prophets and the Other Writings. They believed in baptism of people who confessed their faith in God. And they also believed in the resurrection of the body.

Although some Pharisees made a big show out of their faith, even parading in the streets, many others were quietly prayerful and devout.

Jesus criticized them mainly for their *legalism*—such as their insistence on tithing everything (even sprigs of herbs), their straining of drinking water lest they swallow an impure gnat, and their large gifts to the Temple to the neglect of their needy parents. See *Matthew, ch. 23*, for examples of Jesus' words about such practices.

Still, Jesus did not hesitate to accept dinner invitations from Pharisees. And we can read, in *John, ch. 3*, the interesting story of Nicodemus, a Pharisee who came to visit Jesus by night. Jesus spoke with him about being born again to a new relationship with God.

In the end, the Pharisees mostly condemned Jesus and his ministry.

• The *Sadducees* were another religious party, fewer in number than the Pharisees. These two parties opposed each other.

Sadducees, perhaps dating back to the time of Solomon, were the aristocratic priests who served the Temple and defended the Torah. They disagreed deeply with the Pharisees because they thought only the Torah was needed. They rejected the other codes of law.

Sadducees denied any belief in resurrection, in angels, and in spirits—since none of these was mentioned in the Torah.

But the Sadducees joined with the scribes and Pharisees in opposing Jesus. John the Baptist had spoken the harshest words about them. He said they were a "generation of vipers" *(Matthew, ch. 3)*.

7. Great New Testament Treasures

In our worship, Christians reserve great honor for the Gospels. We stand when the lessons from the Gospel are read at the Eucharist. Why? Because it is from these pages that we hear again and again the central truth of our faith:

Alleluia. Christ is risen.
The Lord is risen indeed. Alleluia.
The resurrection changed everything for Jesus' disci-

ples and for us. Because our Lord lives and reigns, we have hope and joy.

Think, too, about the great lines we sing as Canticles:

• Mary's song, The Magnificat, beginning "My soul magnifies the Lord," from *Luke 1:46-55*.

• The song of Zechariah, father of John the Baptist, beginning "Blessed be the Lord, the God of Israel," from *Luke 1:67-79*.

• The song of Simeon, the aging priest who held the infant Jesus in his arms and said, "Lord, you now have set your servant free to go in peace," from *Luke 2:29-32*.

Through our whole lives, we read and study the story of Jesus. We think about his parables. We trust him as the One who saves and heals us. We give him thanks for his love and forgiveness.

And we join with the writer of the Gospel of John when he supposes "that the world itself could not contain the books that would be written" if we knew everything that Jesus did *(John 21:15)*.

Part III
Holy Baptism

1. Baptism Has a History

After his resurrection from the dead, Jesus instructed his disciples to be baptizers:

"Go therefore and make disciples of all nations, baptizing them in the name of the Father and of the Son and of the Holy Spirit, and teaching them to obey everything that I have commanded you. And remember, I am with you always, to the end of the age." *(Matthew 28:19-20.)*

In obedience to this command from the risen Lord, the Church has baptized millions and millions of people over the last two thousand years. Baptisms take place every week, in every part of the world. They happen in many kinds of congregations.

The baptizing is done by many kinds of ministers, following many different customs. Always, there is water. And always, these words are spoken:

I baptize you, in the Name of the Father, and of the Son, and of the Holy Spirit.

This sentence is called the "baptismal formula." It is the accepted way to welcome people into the Church of Jesus Christ. The words have been translated into every language.

But why is baptism so important to Christians? How did it begin?

In most religions of the world, something like baptism is practiced. Water is used to cleanse and purify, and to serve as a sign to people that they can make a new, fresh beginning in their lives.

Around the time Jesus lived, a group called Essenes had an elaborate water system so that everyone in the community could be washed before their sacred meals.

Among the Pharisees and other Jewish groups, washing was done to welcome new members.

John Baptized Jesus

A new kind of baptizing began with John the Baptist, the son of Elizabeth and Zechariah, who was the one chosen by God to prepare the way for the Messiah. John preached sermons that called on people to "repent"—to turn around and seek forgiveness for their sins. Then he would baptize all who responded to his message, immersing them in the water of the River Jordan.

Jesus was about thirty years old at that time. One day he, too, came to ask for baptism from John. Certainly, Jesus had no need to repent, for he had committed no sin. John said, "No, no, you should be baptizing me!"

Jesus insisted, and so John baptized him. When Jesus came up out of the water, "he saw the heavens torn apart and the spirit descending like a dove on him. And a voice came from heaven, 'You are my Son, the Beloved; with you I am well pleased.'" *(Mark 1:10b-11.)*

That was the beginning of Jesus' own ministry. We celebrate this fact every year on the First Sunday after the Epiphany: The Baptism of our Lord. (See the Collects for this day in *The Book of Common Prayer*, pages 163 or 214.)

In the Gospels, almost nothing more is said about the practice of baptizing. We do not know whether Jesus himself baptized anyone with water. We do not know who baptized the twelve disciples.

Jesus' death and resurrection were followed by a period of waiting. Then the Holy Spirit came upon the apostles at Pentecost, and the Church of Jesus Christ began to grow. Following the Pentecost experience, Peter preached a sermon of great power. His listeners were deeply moved, and they asked what they should do.

Peter said, "Repent, and be baptized." At once, three thousand persons received baptism. (See *Acts 2:37-42*.)

Baptism with water was regarded as a good and necessary way to begin a new life as a follower of the living Christ.

Preparation Required

The Church began, in time, to set requirements for Holy Baptism. It was not enough just to say, "I want to be baptized." Leaders believed people need time to get ready for this sacrament.

In a document named *The Apostolic Tradition of Hippolytus,* we can read about baptismal practices in third-century Rome:

New followers of Jesus Christ were called "catechumens," or "people being taught." They were in training for three years. During that time, they attended worship. Always they sat in a special section reserved for them. But they were not allowed to stay for Holy Eucharist. That privilege was reserved for persons who were already baptized.

At the end of the three years, the catechumens were examined intensely. Did they pray regularly? Did they do good to other people?

On Thursday night before a Sunday baptism, the catechumens bathed themselves as a way of saying, "I am ready." On Friday and Saturday, they ate nothing and prayed earnestly.

An all-night vigil was held on Saturday night. The candidates listened to Scripture and other prayerful readings.

At dawn on Sunday, the congregation met. Some-where, possibly beside a garden pool or fountain, the priest said a prayer over the water.

The candidates then took off all their clothing—to symbolize leaving an old life behind. Children were baptized first. If they could speak for themselves, they did. If not, their parents spoke for them.

Men were baptized next, and then women.

The priest anointed each person with oil that had been blessed by a bishop. This was to drive away evil spirits.

Then the priest asked the catechumens, one by one, if they believed in God the Father, God the Son, and God the Holy Spirit.

After confessing their faith in the three persons of the Trinity, the candidates were completely submerged in the water, three times in all. Then they were anointed with "the oil of thanksgiving."

Each new Christian was dried off, given fresh white garments to wear, and brought to the main place of worship. The bishop laid hands on everyone, praying for the power of the Spirit to come upon them. Then he anointed them once more with the oil of thanksgiving.

The newly-baptized persons were received in the community of Christ's people. They exchanged the peace.

At once, the Eucharist was celebrated. In addition to the bread and the wine, the people received a mixture of milk and honey. This was a sign to the new Christians that God's promise to Israel, long ago, had been fulfilled by Jesus Christ, in his dying and rising again.

After the service, people returned to their homes and their jobs. They did not want to attract attention because many people in Rome were hostile to this new faith.

Through the centuries, the service of baptism has taken many forms. In churches of the East, the baptismal liturgy can be quite long. Sometimes it begins with the children going to the door of the church and spitting to keep the devil away!

In Protestant churches, the service is often simple and short. Some call baptism an "ordinance" instead of a "sacrament." Some churches immerse people in baptisteries built into their buildings. Others perform baptism outdoors in a stream or lake.

Still, there is only *one* baptism. In whatever way we are baptized, in whatever church, our baptism is real and forever. If we become Episcopalians after having belonged to another Christian church, we are not re-baptized.

2. The Sacrament That Is Forever

Baptism is the first of two great *sacraments* given to the Church by Jesus Christ. Sacrament comes from a Latin word that means "holy." It is related to the words "sacred" and "sacrifice."

A sacrament, then, is a holy act in which we express our devotion to God. When we celebrate a sacrament in the Church, we are offering ourselves prayerfully to our Lord.

The sacrament of Holy Eucharist is celebrated again and again. Through our whole lives we can come to the Holy Table and receive the bread and wine, our Lord's body and blood.

But the sacrament of Holy Baptism happens only *once* for each of us. As the water touches us, the bishop or priest says, "I baptize you . . . ." That may happen when we are infants, or it can happen at any other time in our lives.

Whether or not we remember our baptism, it stands always as a sign that we are truly received into the household of God. When we are baptized, we are united with Christ in his death and resurrection, we are born into God's family, our sins are forgiven, and we have a new life in the Holy Spirit.

What we believe about this sacrament is summed up in An Outline of the Faith (Catechism) of *The Book of Common Prayer,* pages 858-859.

Outline of the Service

For Episcopalians, the Prayer Book offers a form for the Service of Holy Baptism that seeks to capture the best of the ancient Christian traditions. It retains a beauty and simplicity that have great appeal.

Following is an outline of the service, with page numbers in parentheses.

1. Acclamation, and *Baptism Versicles* (299).

2. Collect of the Day, Lessons, and *Sermon* (300-301). The sermon may be preached after the Peace instead.

3. Presentation and Examination of the Candidates (301-303). Each person to be baptized, whether an infant or older, is to be presented by one or more sponsors. Sponsors of children are called godparents. Parents and sponsors promise to support and pray for the candidates. They also renounce Satan, evil, and sin—and they promise to accept, trust, and obey Jesus Christ as Lord. The congregation promises to support the candidates in their life in Christ.

4. *The Baptismal Covenant* (304-305). The first part of the Covenant is the Apostles' Creed in the form of three faith questions beginning, "Do you believe . . . ." The five questions that follow are about the actions of a Christian life.

5. *Prayers for the Candidates* (305-306).

6. *Thanksgiving over the Water* (306-307). At this time, if a bishop is present, oil of Chrism may be consecrated (for use when the sign of the cross is made on the forehead of a candidate).

7. *The Baptism* (307-308). The bishop may also confirm persons at the service (309). The Peace is exchanged, and the celebration of Holy Eucharist follows. In cases where the Eucharist is not celebrated, an alternative ending of the service is used (311).

Covenant at the Center

At the very center of the Service of Holy Baptism is The Baptismal Covenant, in which all the church's people confess their faith and promise to live the Christian life.

Covenants are nothing new to God's people. Again and again, God reaches out to us and graciously cares for us. In turn, we promise to be faithful and obedient to God.

We recall the covenants God made with Noah, Abraham and his descendants, and with Moses. And the greatest and last of God's covenants is the New Covenant in Jesus Christ.

So, at every service of Holy Baptism, we *renew* (say again, from the heart) our own Christian covenant.

We begin by answering three faith questions:

Do you believe in God the Father?

Do you believe in Jesus Christ, the Son of God?

Do you believe in God, the Holy Spirit?

Our answers are in the words of the Apostles' Creed. This is believed to be the Church's oldest Creed. It was probably composed in the early Church to be used at baptisms.

As people confessed their faith in the words of the Creed, they could understand the fuller meaning of the baptismal formula, "I baptize you in the Name of the Father, and of the Son, and of the Holy Spirit."

The Baptismal Covenant continues as we reaffirm these promises:

• to take part regularly in the life of the Christian community as it gathers for teaching, Holy Communion, and prayer;

• to resist all forms of evil and sin, and when we fail, to repent and return to the Lord;

• to share the Good News of God in Christ with other people, in both words and actions;

• to serve Christ in other persons, loving our neighbors as ourselves;

• to work for justice and peace in the world, respecting the dignity of every person.

We acknowledge that we cannot keep these promises without the help of God. So we say, in answer to five questions, "I will, with God's help."

3. Believing and Acting

The questions of The Baptismal Covenant remind us that we must not separate what we *believe* from what we *do*. Our belief in God requires that we live a life worthy of God's people.

1. Worship, prayer, and study. The baptized community meets together each Sunday around the Holy Table of our Lord—to join in prayers and to receive the sacrament of Holy Communion. We offer our thanksgiving for all that God has done for us in Jesus Christ, and we resolve to go forth into the world in his name.

As the apostle Paul put it, baptized people are like the parts of a human body. Each part is necessary, and they form a unity. In the same way, each of us is a part of Christ's body. We depend on one another, and we all belong to a holy fellowship.

We treasure the Bible, the Prayer Book, and the long story of God's saints through the centuries. From all these we can learn more and more about the ways of God. We need to read, think, and remember the stories of faith. Through study we gain a deeper understanding of obedience.

2. Resisting evil. It is sadly true that human beings are sinners. We have quarrels and misunderstandings, and we hurt one another's feelings. We do great wrongs to others. We say cruel things. We act selfishly. We abuse our bodies in many ways. We misuse the good gifts God has given us. We waste our time and energy. The list of our failures goes on and on.

On a grand scale, human sin produces national conflict and war. Death, injuries, and terrible suffering follow. When we read the newspapers and listen to the television, we see again and again the results of unrestrained evil in the world.

Each baptized person is called to resist the forces of evil. We have the freedom to say no to temptations.

But when we fail and fall into sinful behavior, we can repent, return to the Lord, and begin a new life. We have been given good news:

God will forgive our sins if we are faithful to confess them. We can trust in God's love and mercy.

3. Sharing our faith. Baptized people have the wonderful privilege of sharing the good news of Jesus Christ with other people. We share not only by the words we speak but also by the example of our daily living.

If we think of the persons we admire most in the Christian church, we recall the pleasant words they have spoken to us, the kind things they have done for us, and the ways they have demonstrated their deep commitment to our Lord. Their faith is contagious.

Baptized people do not hide their faith and love from others. In quiet and helpful ways, they reach out to family members, friends, neighbors, and strangers. Their words and their deeds help other people to feel welcome in the great community of Christian believers.

4. Seeking and serving Christ in others. All the people we meet at school, at work, or wherever we go, are our neighbors. It may not be easy to think of everyone in that way, but we do know that God made us all.

People are from all age groups, they come from many races and nations, and they have a wide variety of languages and customs. But one thing they have in common: they were all made by God, and each one is a child of God for whom Christ died.

Baptized people give help and comfort to their neighbors. When persons are in trouble or in need, Christians come to their aid. When people are lonely or lost, Christians offer friendship and guidance.

Jesus described a day when he would appear as a king, saying, " . . . I was hungry and you gave me food, I was thirsty and you gave me something to drink, I was a stranger and you welcomed me, I was naked and you gave me clothing, I was sick and you took care of me, I was in prison and you visited me." *(Matthew 25:35-36.)*

Righteous people would ask the king, "When did we do all these things for you?"

And the Lord would answer, "Truly I tell you, just as you did it to one of the least of these who are members of my family, you did it to me." *(Matthew 25:40.)*

When we do good for other people, it is as if we are doing it for Jesus.

5. Working for justice and peace. We know what it is like to be treated unfairly. It is important to have someone take our side and help us to put things right again. We do not like unjust treatment.

We want *justice,* not just for ourselves but for everyone.

We also know how it feels when a friend stops speaking to us. We wish so much that everything could be the way it was! We do not like to have enemies.

We want *peace,* not just for ourselves but for everyone.

Baptized people are called to work for justice and peace in our homes, in our schools, in our work, and in our play.

We can do a lot to be peacemakers and champions of justice just by becoming well informed. If we listen to all sides in an argument, we can help to sort out the truth and settle the disagreements. If we forgive the people who hurt us and reach out to them in friendship and love, we may be surprised by a wonderful sense of peace.

We remember this duty to seek good relations with others every time we pass the Peace at the Holy Eucharist. We say to the people around us, "The peace of the Lord be with you." This is our way of declaring that we are all forgiven sinners who need one another very, very much. We respect the dignity of each person.

4. Great Truth, Great Symbols

If Jesus Christ had not been raised from the dead, there would have been no Church. We would not call ourselves Christians.

We can rejoice that our Lord did win a victory over death. The tomb could not hold him, and he lives "at the right hand of the Father."

The sacrament of Holy Baptism is like a drama that helps people to remember what God accomplished in Jesus Christ.

Among the symbols associated with baptism, three are especially meaningful:

1. Water. Water means everything to us when we are thirsty, and it is a sign of life and growth for all plant and animal life. To be without water in a great drought is to know real suffering.

It is also true that water can be very dangerous. A flood can rush upon us and destroy our homes, our crops, and our very own lives. Sailors can tell terrifying stories about storms on the open sea when water piles into high waves and threatens to drown everything in its path. Deep streams and rivers with strong currents can be perilous to navigate.

Think, then, about these opposites:

Water can mean life.

Water can mean death.

The apostle Paul had those opposites in mind when he wrote to the Christians at Rome, "Do you not know that all of us who have been baptized into Christ Jesus were baptized into his death? Therefore we have been buried with him by baptism into death, so that, just as Christ was raised from the dead by the glory of the Father, so we too might walk in newness of life." *(Romans 6:3-4.)*

For Paul, baptism was done by immersion in water. The water was dangerous, even deathly, unless the persons being baptized were lifted up so that they could breathe again. So, being lowered into the water was a symbol of Christ's death. Being raised up out of the water was a symbol of Christ's resurrection!

In the drama of baptism, life wins out over death. That is the good news of the Christian faith: Christ has died. But Christ is risen!

To be baptized is to experience both death and resurrection. Because our Lord lives, we shall live. That is our faith.

2. Light. It is hard for us to imagine what it would be like not to have light. We understand very well the contrast between light and darkness:

Light forever means life.

Darkness forever means death.

So it does not surprise us that Jesus spoke of himself as "the light of the world." He said, "I have come as light into the world, so that everyone who believes in me should not remain in the darkness." *(John 12:46.)*

By being light forever, Jesus Christ overcomes the death of darkness.

The Easter Vigil (the evening before Easter Day) is a brilliant drama about the risen Christ as light.

As the service begins, the church is in darkness. A paschal (Easter) candle is prepared, lighted, and carried in procession. A bishop or priest proclaims, "The light of Christ!"

Then the Easter baptisms take place by the light of the paschal candle. All through the year, when a baptism occurs, this lighted candle is present. It is a symbol of the new life given to each of us in this sacrament of initiation into Christ's body, the Church.

In Eastern churches, to this day, a white garment is placed on each person being baptized. It is called the "robe of light," linking the sacrament of baptism with Christ as light of the world.

In many Episcopal churches, a baptismal candle is lighted from the paschal candle and presented to the parents of a newly baptized child. Families treasure the baptismal candle as a sign of the light of Christ in their homes. Sometimes parents will re-light the baptismal candle for a few minutes each year, on the anniversary of their child's baptism.

3. Dove. When Jesus was baptized by John, in the Jordan River, the Holy Spirit descended upon him "like a dove."

Then "a voice came from heaven, 'You are my Son, the Beloved; with you I am well pleased.'" *(Mark 1:11.)*

The early Church understood that "the Beloved" was God's anointed one, the Messiah. So this was wonderful good news to the world: Jesus is the one God had promised to send as Savior for all humankind!

In paintings, tapestries, stained glass windows, and banners, the dove stands for the Spirit's message about Jesus. Wherever we see this symbol, we are reminded that we are united with Jesus forever through our baptism.

The priest makes the sign of the cross on the forehead of a person being baptized, saying, "You are sealed by the Holy Spirit in Baptism and marked as Christ's own for ever."

We are baptized by water and the Spirit.

5. Welcome!

When we are baptized and take our places as members of the Church, we become "ministers."

That strikes most of us as startling news. We know about bishops, priests, and deacons. But how could we *all* be called ministers?

Turn, in *The Book of Common Prayer,* to An Outline of the Faith (Catechism), page 855:

Question: Who are the ministers of the Church?
Answer: The ministers of the Church are lay persons, bishops, priests, and deacons.

"Lay persons" are listed first. "Lay" comes from a Greek word that means "the whole people of God." Every baptized person belongs to the great body of lay persons, also known as "the laity."

If we go on to read the next question, we discover what kind of ministers the lay persons are expected to be:

Question: What is the ministry of the laity?
Answer: The ministry of lay persons is to represent Christ and his Church; to bear witness to him wherever they may be; and, according to the gifts given them, to carry on Christ's work of reconciliation in the world; and to take their place in the life, worship, and governance of the Church.

It has been said that our baptism is our ordination to the "first order" of ministry. The other orders are those of bishops, priests, and deacons. Everyone who is baptized takes on the responsibility to be one of Christ's followers in the world—reaching out to others in the ways we promise to do in The Baptismal Covenant.

At the end of the Service of Holy Baptism, the Celebrant says, "Let us welcome the newly baptized."

The congregation—all the lay ministers assembled in the church—will then say the following to the baptized persons: "We receive you into the household of God. Confess the faith of Christ crucified, proclaim his resurrection, and share with us in his eternal priesthood."

This challenging word of *welcome* is an invitation to share in Christ's ministry. So it is important for us all to help people feel truly welcome and at home in their chosen church:

• We can learn the names of all the people in our congregation so that we can greet them, get acquainted, and learn about their accomplishments and pleasures, and also their disappointments and times of sadness.

- We can find out about people's gifts and talents. If persons have speaking ability, they can learn to read at the Church's services. If they have musical gifts, they can sing in choirs or play instruments for various groups. If they like to be with children, we can invite them to work in the Christian education program.

- We can make telephone calls, write notes, and visit people in their homes—to let them know we are thinking of them and care about their joys and sorrows.

These are only a few of the simple ways we can assist in helping persons to feel wanted, needed, and privileged as members of a caring, loving Christian congregation.

In earlier times, "family Bibles" were a treasured possession in many Christians' homes. Often they were quite large with big print. In the center would be several pages for keeping family records. One page was likely to be headed "Baptisms." Here would be a list of the names of family members, together with the dates and places of their baptisms.

Such Bibles are not as popular today. But if they were, we would be glad to see our own names on the Baptism pages, along with our brothers and sisters, mother and father, grandparents, and others. As we looked at the list and thought about the passing years, we could be grateful again for the sacrament of Holy Baptism—remembering the opening line of a prayer in the Service:

"Heavenly Father, we thank you that by water and the Holy Spirit you have bestowed upon these your servants the forgiveness of sin, and have raised them to the new life of grace. . . ." *(The Book of Common Prayer,* page 308.)

PART IV
Paul

1. How Paul Became a Christian

Paul was a great pioneer of the early Church. His travels, his preaching, and his writing helped to shape the whole history of the Christian faith.

More than half of Luke's book, The Acts of the Apostles, is about Paul's life and the journeys he made. Letters Paul wrote to the churches he founded are the oldest part of the New Testament. They were written before the four Gospels. About one-fifth of the New Testament was written by Paul.

But this remarkable man was not always a follower of Jesus Christ. At first, he was just the opposite—a fierce opponent of the Christians.

Paul was born a Roman citizen at Tarsus, in Cilicia. His name at birth was Saul, and he was probably from a leading Hebrew family. They may have been wealthy.

As a young adult, Saul took up the trade of tent making (or leather working) in order to support himself while he concentrated on learning Jewish law. He went to Jerusalem to study with a famous rabbi named Gamaliel. There he heard about the growing number of Jewish people who had become followers of the Way. They accepted Jesus as the long-expected Messiah, and they claimed he had risen from the dead.

Saul believed the members of this new group were all wrong. He felt quite sure their leaders should be severely punished.

He had no sympathy for a follower of Christ named Stephen, who was becoming one of the well-known leaders of the Way. Stephen had upset many Jewish leaders. This Stephen was brought before a council and charged with spreading false teaching. When Stephen stood up and declared his faith in Jesus of Nazareth as the risen Lord, the council leaders were enraged. They condemned Stephen to death by stoning.

As Stephen faced his accusers, they threw off their outer garments and rushed toward him with stones in their hands. Before he died, he prayed, "Lord, do not hold this sin against them."

Saul was standing there, with the men's clothing lying on the ground at his feet. He did nothing to stop what happened, for he believed the council was right.

Blinded on the Road

The persecution of Christ's followers continued, and Saul himself was "breathing threats and murder against the disciples of the Lord." Around the year 33 CE, he asked the high priest for letters to the synagogues at Damascus so that he could go there and round up anyone still belonging to the Way (both men and women). He would bind them and bring them to Jerusalem. *(Acts 9:1.)*

On the road to Damascus, Saul's whole life was changed!

He was overcome by a great light, and he heard a voice saying, "Saul, Saul, why do you persecute me?" It was Jesus! Saul fell to the ground. The people with him heard the voice, but they saw nothing.

When Saul stood, he could not see. His companions led him on to Damascus. For three days he could not see, and he had nothing to eat or drink.

A Christian leader named Ananias had a vision concerning Saul. The Lord told Ananias that Saul was to become a Christian missionary.

When Ananias went to the house where Saul was, he welcomed him as a brother and told him that his sight would be restored. He would also receive the gift of the Holy Spirit.

Immediately, something like scales fell from Paul's eyes. He could see again! At once, he was baptized. Christians in Damascus continued to care for him several days longer.

Now Saul was in a strange position. The Jewish leaders heard him speaking about Jesus as the Christ, and they plotted to kill him. He went back to Jerusalem, but he found that the followers of the Way were afraid of him. Could they trust this man who had been their enemy?

A follower named Barnabas defended Saul. Barnabas arranged to send him to Tarsus.

We do not know very much about how Paul spent the next twelve or fourteen years. He changed his name to Paul and continued to preach the good news of Jesus Christ. Three years after his conversion, he went to Jerusalem to visit Peter, who had become the leader of the Church. He stayed fifteen days but did not meet any of the other apostles at that time. (See *Galatians 1:11-24*.)

He called himself an "apostle." This term was later reserved for the twelve disciples (the eleven faithful ones Jesus chose, plus Matthias who was selected, to replace Judas Iscariot, the betrayer). These were the ones who had seen Jesus in person and had been witnesses to the resurrection. Paul insisted that the experience on the road to Damascus qualified him to be considered an apostle, too.

2. Paul Traveled Widely

Paul is remembered for his extensive travel. He became a missionary for Christ, and he helped to begin new communities of Christians over a very wide territory. Many Bibles are published with a set of maps at the back. Usually, one of these is labeled "The Journeys of Paul," and it helps us to trace the routes Paul followed.

Below is a listing of the places Paul visited on his three long journeys. An asterisk (*) follows each place to which a New Testament letter of Paul was addressed. (Within parentheses after these places, names of Paul's letters are printed in italics. Note that Paul visited some of these cities more than once.)

- The first journey, from 46-48 CE, is described in *Acts 13:1* through *14:20*. It was devoted to the region of Asia Minor.

With Barnabas and John Mark, Paul started out from Antioch in Syria. Over the next two years he visited Seleucia, Salamis, Paphos, and Perga. John Mark went home from Perga. Paul and Barnabas continued to Antioch of Pisidia, Iconium, Lystra, and Derbe.

Then they returned to Lystra, Iconium, Antioch of Pisidia, and Perga (in that order).

On the way back to Antioch in Syria, they stopped in Attalia.

- The second journey, from 49-51 CE, can be traced in *Acts 15:36* through *18:22*. Paul introduced the Christian faith to Macedonia (which we know as southern Europe).

This time Paul's companion was Silas. The journey began and ended at Antioch in Syria. They went to Syria, Cilicia, Derbe, and Lystra (where young Timothy joined them).

The next stops were Troas, Philippi* *(Philippians)*, Thessalonica* *(I and II Thessalonians)*, and Beroea. Silas remained behind while Paul went on to Athens and Corinth* *(I and II Corinthians)*. Silas and Timothy rejoined Paul in Corinth, and they traveled to Ephesus* *(Ephesians)*, Caesarea, and back to Jerusalem.

- The third journey, from 52-56 CE, is found in *Acts 18:23* through *21:16*. Paul had hoped to press on to Rome, but he was not able to do so on this trip.

Once again, he started from Antioch in Syria. He traveled to Galatia* *(Galatians)*, Phrygia, Ephesus, Troas, Philippi, Thessalonica, Beroea, and Corinth.

Then he went back to Philippi and Troas. From there he ventured to Miletus and Tyre, and on to Caesarea and Jerusalem.

Just following the routes on a map can be an interesting exercise. What is important is the fact that Paul made friends wherever he went. He preached the gospel, baptized new believers, and helped to strengthen the small Christian communities that were forming all across the Mediterranean world.

Luke, the Gospel writer, was one of Paul's companions during part of his travels. Perhaps he kept a diary. If so, that would explain all the details provided in The Acts of the Apostles.

Means of Transportation

Paul's travels were thrilling at times. He was undertaking a very dangerous mission, for transportation in those days was very slow and perilous. Still, Paul covered many hundreds of miles.

He may have ridden camels and mules in caravans.

Richer people were sometimes carried on a litter held on the shoulders of slaves. Paul probably also used carts, chariots, and carriages of various kinds. When he traveled by sea, he would take a galley ship with sails and oarsmen.

Paul's friends may have helped to pay his travel expenses. Part of the time he earned money at a loom making cloth for use in tents. No doubt he sometimes had no money at all and had to walk from place to place.

One thing is sure. If it had not been for Paul's persistent labor, the Christian message would not have taken root in the way it did. We can be very grateful for his courage.

3. The Last Trip

After Paul's third missionary journey, he went to the temple in Jerusalem to fulfill a vow. People who opposed his ministry found out he was there, and they charged him with being an unfaithful Jew, an enemy of their faith.

In fury, a mob of people formed to attack Paul. His life was saved by Roman soldiers who rushed in to protect him. Paul then stood on the stairs of the castle and spoke in Hebrew. He defended himself in a long speech as his Jewish brothers listened. But it did no good. Their anger was even greater.

The Roman officer, not understanding why Paul was being attacked so furiously, was determined to scourge him until he explained.

But Paul spoke up and claimed his rights as a Roman citizen by birth. He appealed his case to Caesar, the emperor.

As a result, Paul was sent to Caesarea to the Roman governor, Felix, for a hearing.

Felix did nothing about Paul's situation for two years. He simply kept him in prison while hoping Paul would give him some money.

Then Felix was succeeded by Festus, who was determined to settle the case. King Agrippa of Judea arrived on a visit to welcome Festus as the new governor. Festus told Agrippa all about Paul, and the king agreed to see the prisoner for himself.

Paul made an eloquent speech to Agrippa, who concluded that he could have been set free if he had not already appealed to Rome. Instead, he was sent on his way to that great city. He was bound as a prisoner and accompanied by a guard named Julius who treated him kindly.

The story of Paul's last recorded trip is described dramatically in *Acts 27:1* through *28:16*. The route took him to Sidon, Cyprus, Myra, Crete, Fair Havens, Phoenix, Malta, Syracuse, Rhegium, Puteoli, the Forum off Appius, and The Three Taverns. This account of Paul's harrowing experience on the sea, including a shipwreck, is one of the most exciting travel tales we have. It causes us to hold our breath as we read it for the first time!

Once Paul arrived in Rome, he was allowed to stay by himself, with only his guard. For two years he paid his own expenses (59-61 CE). See *Acts 28:30*.

4. Paul Wrote Letters

The New Testament contains thirteen letters that bear Paul's name. Nine, possibly ten, of these were almost certainly written by Paul himself. They are the oldest books of the Christian Scriptures.

The three or four additional letters may have been written by others, with Paul's name added. (This was not an unusual practice in those days.)

Paul would probably be quite surprised to discover that his letters are in the Bible. He wrote them because people in the churches needed help or needed to be taught, and each letter had its own purpose. But he would surely not be sorry that the whole world can read his strong testimonies for the power of God in Christ.

When Paul wanted to send a letter, he would ask for a public letter-writer, or a friend. Then he would dictate his message. Only one of his secretaries is mentioned by name. He was Tertius *(Romans 16:22)*.

The letter-writer, or scribe, would use a pen made of reed, brownish ink, and sheets of papyrus.

Scholars of the Bible believe the letters were written in the following order, with the dates (CE) in parentheses:

1. ***First Thessalonians*** (50). This letter is the first piece of writing in our New Testament.

On Paul's visit to Thessalonica (during the second journey), he was able to stay only about three weeks because of opposition from enemies. After he left, he was anxious about the new followers of Christ in that place, so he sent Timothy back to find out how they were. Paul waited for news, first at Athens and then at Corinth.

When Timothy returned, he reported that the church was faithful in spite of everything their enemies did to discourage them. So Paul wrote his thanks for the good news. He also defended his own character as an apostle, and he shared the fact that he was working with his own hands to make tentcloth and earn money. Paul also urged the Thessalonians to wait for Christ's second coming with comfort and hope.

2. ***Second Thessalonians*** (50). Paul sent this letter very soon after the first one. Some people in the church at Thessalonica were so sure the Lord's second coming was at hand that they had stopped working. In their idleness, they engaged in bad behavior.

Paul wrote some strong advice: "Anyone unwilling to work should not eat." *(II Thessalonians 3:10b.)*

3. *Galatians* (52). Probably while he was at home in Antioch of Syria, following his second journey, Paul learned that a segment of Christian leaders were insisting that Gentiles who wanted to become Christians must first become practicing Jews.

Paul was determined to write a response to this kind of teaching. He wrote a letter to the Christians at Galatia which has been called a "declaration of freedom." He said that the Church of Jesus Christ is open to all persons—not only Jews but everyone. Paul wanted the Christian faith to be a world religion that welcomed all races and nations.

The letter calls on Christians to accept the freedom they have been given by God. It is a gracious gift, not something earned.

4. *First Corinthians* (53-55). On his second journey, Paul had spent more than a year at the city of Corinth. Scholars believe he may have written as many as four letters to the church there, and that the two we have in the New Testament are pieced together from all four.

Paul was concerned about immoral living in Corinth. The Christians there sent him a list of questions asking about problems in their congregation. For example, what were they to do about cliques among the members? What were they to do about meat that had been sacrificed to idols? How were they to conduct their worship? Paul wrote his forthright and helpful responses.

Some famous passages in the First Letter are *ch. 11:23-26,* which includes the words instituting the

Eucharist; *ch. 13,* on Christian love; and *ch. 15,* on resurrection of the dead.

5. *Second Corinthians* (53-55). In the first section of this letter, Paul gives thanks to the Corinthian Christians, who feel more hospitable toward him now. He has learned that things are better in the church there, and apparently he has recovered from an illness.

At this time, Paul was gathering an offering for poor Christians in Jerusalem. In this letter, he urges the Corinthians to give generously. (See also *I Corinthians 16:2-4* and *Romans 15:25.*)

The last part of the letter, which does not seem connected to the other parts, is addressed to people who have not been loyal and have hurt his feelings. He wants to convince them that he is worthy to be their minister in Christ.

6. *Romans* (55). While Paul was in Corinth, he hoped to go to Rome, which was the very center of world affairs. He wanted to go on to Spain from there.

Probably Paul would go to the docks and watch the ships sailing for Rome. It would be tempting to get on board. But he knew he must go first to Jerusalem to deliver an offering he was gathering for needy people. (See *II Corinthians 8:1-15.*)

So Paul had to settle for writing a letter to the church in Rome. It is not so much a personal message, for it sounds like an essay describing his understanding of the Christian faith and what it asks us to do. (See Section 5 of this Treasurebook.)

7. *Philippians* (59-61). Written while he was a prisoner in Rome, probably not long before he was mar-

tyred, this letter of Paul is addressed to the church at Philippi. It was the first Christian congregation in Europe, and Paul had some dear friends there. They may have been paying for his lodging in Rome.

The Philippians, when they heard about Paul's life in Rome, sent one of their members named Epaphroditis to take him money.

After a while, Epaphroditis became very sick. News of this would have traveled back to the Philippians, causing them to worry. So Paul sent him back, when he was able to make the trip. He took this letter with him. It is a thank-you note. But more than that, it contains some of Paul's most joyous declarations of faith, such as "I press on toward the goal for the prize of the heavenly call of God in Christ Jesus" *(ch. 3:14)*.

8. *Colossians* (59-61). During Paul's two years in Rome, he was permitted to stay in a house that he rented. He was guarded by Roman soldiers while awaiting his trial. The house became a sort of missionary headquarters, as Paul spoke of his faith to the soldiers and to other Christians in Rome. He was staying in touch with Timothy, Luke, and Mark.

One letter he wrote while in prison was sent to the church at Colossae, about a hundred miles east of Ephesus.

Paul had not been there, but he had talked with Epaphras, the founder of the Colossian congregation. Epaphras brought news of strange ideas that had crept into the faith of his church (observing of mysteries, festivals, and various regulations).

Paul wrote a letter to combat these errors. He wanted the Colossians to know that they needed only to believe in Christ. Faith in him is all that really matters.

Paul sent Tychicus to deliver this important letter.

9. *Philemon* (59-61). When Paul sent Tychicus to Colossae with a letter to the congregation, he also sent another short letter to Philemon, one of the church's members.

Philemon's slave, Onesimus, had run away to Rome. While there, he had met Paul and become a Christian. He knew then that he should return to his master, but how could he face the severe punishment, which might even be death?

Paul wrote a plea to Philemon, asking him to take Onesimus back and accept him as a brother in Christ. Onesimus could confess his wrongdoing and prove he could be trusted. The letter shows Paul to be a man with a pastor's heart.

Since Tychicus was making the trip with the two letters, Onesimus traveled with him.

10. *Ephesians* (59-61?). One writer has said that Paul's letter to the Ephesians is always "like an important message that arrived in the morning mail." It is about Christian unity. People have one Father who is loving; they should be like brothers and sisters under one Lord.

Scholars of the New Testament do not agree about who wrote Ephesians. Some believe Paul wrote it from prison in Rome, about the same time as the letter to the Colossians. Others offer reasons to believe it was written by someone else. It was sent as a circular letter to a number of different churches.

Ephesians contains a wonderful description of the church as the body of Christ, with ministers serving different functions. (See *ch. 4*.)

Three letters that bear Paul's name are called "pastoral." They are addressed to pastors of Christian congregations, but they also speak to other Christians.

Scholars are not agreed about the dates for the pastoral letters. Some believe that Paul wrote them himself, from Rome. Others think they may have been composed from Paul's notes. Possibly a majority of Biblical researchers believe all three were written by someone else, much later, with the addition of Paul's name.

11. *First Timothy* (after 100?). The writer gives suggestions about public worship, and instructions on how to be a good leader and a good follower in the Church.

12. *Second Timothy* (after 100?). This letter appeals for guarding the truth of the Christian gospel, and for being faithful readers of Scripture. The final verses *(ch. 4:6-22)* are probably fragments of Paul's actual correspondence.

13. *Titus* (after 100?). This letter gives a pastor instruction about leaders in the church, and about Christian behavior in the world.

The letters of Paul do not appear in the Bible in the order in which they were written (as outlined above). Rather, they seem to be arranged in the New Testament according to their length. The longest (Romans) is first, and the shortest (Philemon) is last.

The words of greeting and closing are typical of Paul. In seven of his letters, after stating to whom he is writing, he adds, "Grace to you and peace from God our Father and the Lord Jesus Christ." The other letters have a similar greeting, with slight variations.

Most of the letters end with a form of "Grace be with you." Sometimes Paul would add a final sentence or more in his own handwriting. See, for example, *I Corinthians 16:21*.

5. Paul Explained Christian Faith

More than any other New Testament writer, Paul was careful to spell out his understanding of the Christian faith. He used key words in a special way, and he became the Church's first great theologian (one who describes the work of God).

Following is a short list of ideas and words Paul used, together with brief definitions:

Cross of Christ. This came to mean much more than just the wood on which Christ died. The cross stands for Christ's giving himself up to humiliation and death. For Christian believers, his dying opens the way to forgiveness and salvation from God.

Gospel of Christ. Gospel means good news. Even though we are sinners, God loves us and reaches out to us in love. This is the good news that came to us in Jesus Christ.

Sin. To sin is to rebel against God, and to be separated from God because of this rebellion. Sins are actions of people who do not wish to be obedient to God.

Law. The Torah, or teachings of God, contained God's law for the Hebrew people. Paul was able to see that obeying this law in all its details could not make a person right with God. Something more was needed—the grace and freedom found in the Christian gospel.

God's grace. This term refers to the unlimited and merciful goodness of God, given freely to humankind. It is God's gift of the very finest that can be received even when no one deserves it. Our own goodness is not enough. God must, and does, help us.

Faith. Christians believe that God acted in Jesus Christ to offer salvation to humankind. Faith is putting one's whole trust in God, with total confidence that the gospel of Christ is true.

Justification by faith. A person who puts complete trust in God is set into a right relationship with God. Having faith in Christ assures us that God establishes us in "righteousness." This rightness with God is not something we can create for ourselves; God offers it to us as a gift.

Salvation. This is the term for being admitted into a new life in Jesus Christ. Salvation is a process of being saved from sin and death, and being raised up to live in a different way as a child of God. We are saved by our *faith,* and not by our own efforts to please God.

Righteousness. To stand before God and other people in a state of "rightness" is a gift from God. Whatever works for God's purpose is righteous; whatever interferes with God's purpose is wrong.

All these words and ideas are closely related to one another. Paul used them in his Letter to the Romans. He wanted the Christians there to be strong in their faith and to understand that God had acted on their behalf to offer them a new life in Christ.

By reading Paul's letters we can find out what the early Church taught and preached. In every generation, as we hear his words read aloud in worship, they tell us how the Church should respond to the good news of Jesus Christ.

6. What Finally Happened to Paul?

None of the churches Paul began is in existence today. Most of the cities he visited have disappeared as well. Still, miraculously, his letters remain. They have been read in every country in the world, translated into many hundreds of languages.

But what happened to Paul in the end? During his two years of house arrest in Rome, he was waiting for a trial. Did it happen? And what was the verdict?

No one knows the answers to these questions. Perhaps Luke meant to write a third book that would tell us.

People have speculated that Paul was released after his first trial in Rome and took a fourth missionary journey. Perhaps he wrote the pastoral letters as a result of that trip. Perhaps he went back to Ephesus and left Timothy in charge of the church there.

He may have gone to Macedonia where he could have written his first letter to Timothy. One legend suggests that Paul went to the island of Crete and started a church. Could Titus have been the pastor of that congregation?

Finally, according to some legends, Paul was arrested a second time and returned to prison in Rome, where he wrote his second letter to Timothy.

None of these theories can be proven. Many scholars believe Paul met his death as a martyr right after his trial in 61 BC. While the circumstances remain unknown, everyone agrees that Paul was condemned and died by beheading.

7. What Kind of Man Was Paul?

The traditional shield for the apostle Paul has an open Bible placed over a sword. On the Bible is the Latin inscription, "Spiritus gladius." This means "Sword of the Spirit."

Another symbol for Paul is two crossed swords—one standing for his "good fight of faith," and the other standing for his martyrdom by the sword. Other emblems for Paul are the armor of God and a palm tree.

Paul was a person sure of himself. He knew that God had acted powerfully in his life, and he was never uncertain about the reality of Jesus Christ.

He did not shy away from saying what he believed. This led him into conflict with authorities. People sometimes thought he was mentally unbalanced. But none of his troubles prevented him from praying and singing. He sang hymns in jail.

Paul had many friends. Wherever he went, he could count on someone to provide a place for him to stay. He must have been a fascinating house guest. People would come in great numbers to hear him explain the Christian faith. One time he preached so long in a house that a young man went to sleep and fell out the window!

He was a person who had peace in his heart. One day he could be hungry and another day well fed. One day he might face tumultuous crowds and angry accusers. Another day he might be received as a celebrity. But he had learned, he said, to be contented regardless of his circumstances. He believed that "all things work together for good for those who love God . . . ." *(Romans 8:28a)*.

He believed that God in Christ had broken down all

the walls that separate people. So it is up to Christians to demonstrate to the world that these barriers no longer have power to separate us from one another.

Slaves and free people, men and women, Jews and Gentiles—all are equal in the sight of God, Paul declared. The good news of salvation can be proclaimed freely to all. Certainly Paul was a hard worker. He drove himself to exhaustion on his journeys. Still, one gets the impression that he found a special joy in sharing the gospel to so wide a circle. He never lost the vision of Christianity as a faith for the whole world rather than just another sect.

He was not perfect, he was human. He could sometimes write with anger, sarcasm, and bitterness. See especially his Letter to the Galatians. Sometimes the rules he made for the churches seemed harsh and unduly restrictive.

Still, we can never doubt that he always had the best interests of the Christian churches at heart. He was not looking over his shoulder to wonder what people would think of him in hundreds of years. He lived for the time in which he served his Lord, to whom he was passionately committed.

NOTES

NOTES

NOTES